Evernote for Your Productivity

The Beginner's Guide to Getting Things Done with Evernote
~ or ~
How to Organize Your Life with Note-taking and Archiving

Table of Contents

Introduction

In this day and age, life is a complicated affair, and the notion of keeping track of everything has increasingly become a full-time job in and of itself. Our days are comprised of a strafe of phone calls and emails, TV and social media, work, meetings, family, kids, meals; never-ending sources of information and a constant barrage of things to remember. Each piece demands a place in our life and in our minds. Just writing it out can make your head spin, and naturally, the resulting frustration and stress leads most of us to lose ourselves in the onslaught. We've all had those weeks (or months, or years) where we are just begging ourselves to find some kind of balance and organization in the mess. But the big question is: How? Organizing your life would be an easy job, if you lived in the 1800s, but the fast-paced world of today can rapidly leave you behind, or just drown you.

As this assault of information continues, the size of our hard drives inflates to keep up. From megabytes to gigabytes and beyond; now terabytes have become the norm. In this gigantic heap of documents and media, finding that file you saved a few months ago is a daunting prospect, and that old English proverb "finding a needle in a hay stack" is given all new virtual meaning.

Our brains are just not designed to handle this bombardment of information, and the resulting disorder leaves most of us perplexed. This leaves us crying, "Where's the way out?"   The silver lining in all of this is that we are not alone. This is continuously affecting everybody. But that doesn't help much does it? How is that a silver lining?

Here is where Evernote comes to the rescue. Demand creates supply, and the developers at **Evernote.com** have developed the exact solution to all of these problems. Ever thought of just extracting all your thoughts and storing them somewhere safe? Evernote presents a way to do just that. Now you can transfer all the things that you need to remember, store, or save for the future to one platform. Using cloud storage technology, Evernote applications provide accessibility across multiple platforms. From your desktop or laptop and your favorite web browsers to your handheld devices, you can access all your data with one single account, from any device, anytime, anywhere.

Moreover, Evernote just celebrated its sixth anniversary, which bears a strong testimony to its success and its secure future. With its continuous updates and developments to fulfill users' demands, the advantages offered are just incredible and fully capable of revolutionizing your life. Evernote presents a powerful solution that makes everything in your digital world just a click away. And the great news is, Evernote is not only a multipurpose storage space for your information, but also features a slick creation mode for writing new documents to present directly in the application when desired.

With this much usability to offer, it's up to you to decide: **Are you ready to redesign your life with Evernote?**

Chapter1 - Why Evernote?

Find Anything, Anytime, Anywhere

Evernote has its own OCR (Optical Character Recognition) service, which means that it can read text, whether it's keyboard text, text in a PDF document, a photocopy of some text (say a page of a book), or even text in a photograph. If you are in a photo, standing in front of a plane that says "U.S. Air Force" for example, or any other identifying marks, Evernote's OCR function will read the words and make those words searchable in your account.

If you are wearing a t-shirt that says "makeuseof.com," that URL becomes readable and searchable. Never again will you have to waste time typing an identifying phrase.

Email All Important Documents & Photos with Your Unique Evernote Email Address

Evernote provides all users with their own unique email address. You can use this address to automatically forward important emails, files, photos, other attachments, and even newsletters that you want to save without clogging up your email quota.

If you're simply a careful person, use your personal Evernote email address to send a backup of anything you want, just in case.

Have Access to All Your Stored Documents & Files Wherever You Go

With well-built apps that are a pleasure to use for the computer desktop, iPad, iPhone, and Android, you can access your files anywhere you go. Everything is automatically synchronized so you can use Evernote to carry your study notes and textbooks if you're a student. If you're a teacher or professor, you can carry exam papers and class plans.

Career professionals can scan and carry important trade journals, research papers and presentations. Grocery shoppers can put their shopping lists and recipes on Evernote and access them via their smartphone or iPad in the supermarket. Whoever you are and whatever you do, you can find a use for completely dispensing with paper and storing everything on Evernote.

Leave Voice Notes

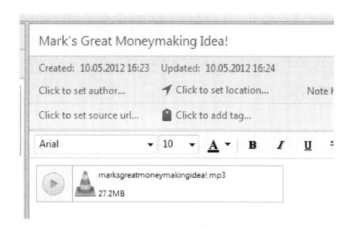

Fig 1.1A Voice note example in Evernote

Evernote allows you to leave voice notes which are also searchable. Using the various smartphone apps, you can speak your note into your phone, and the note is then saved to your account and synchronized to all other instances of Evernote that you have installed on your computers and smart devices.

So if you're out and about and a great idea strikes, don't bother looking for a napkin and pen. Just phone it in to Evernote!

Create Your Own Digital Scrapbook

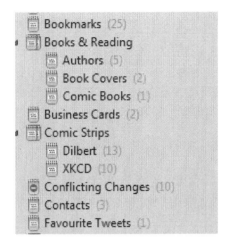

Fig 1.2 Evernote's Categories Menu

Create up to 250 notebooks and organize your online digital life. Subcategorize and tag each one so you can find them easily. Now when you want to put something quickly in a notebook, open that notebook up and drag your image or file directly into the notebook area.

Store & Synchronize Your Browser Bookmarks

Enter the URL of the article you want to keep. Transfer all of your browser bookmarks over to Evernote categorized and tagged, so your browser can run faster. There's no need to use the browser to store your bookmarks ever again. Put them in Evernote and synchronize them across all platforms and operating systems. Copy and paste images into the note to remind yourself what the URL is all about and why you initially bookmarked it.

Notebook Sharing

With Evernote, you can collaborate with others and show people what you have in your notebooks (provided you have a premium subscription). If you are working on a project together, throw the required files/notes into a notebook and share them, or make the notebook publicly available so anyone can see it. You can work on text together with a friend or colleague – perfect for preparing a presentation together.

"Evernote Free" vs. "Evernote Premium" – Should You Upgrade?

Whether or not you upgrade to Evernote Premium will depend on your usage of the service. Basically, premium users, like myself, are obsessive digital hoarders and so the 60MB that Evernote currently provides to all free users per month simply doesn't cut it.

But if you are a very casual user and you don't see yourself going over the 60MB limit, you can quite easily use Evernote for free forever. Just try using the service for a couple of months to see how close to the limit you get before deciding whether or not to get your money out for an upgrade.

If you decide to upgrade, there ARE advantages to a paid plan:

- **Your monthly data limit is raised** from **60MB to 1GB**. That's over **sixteen and a half times more** space. And it's very probable that, at some point in the future, Evernote will raise those limits when it becomes feasible and cost-effective to do so.
- **Access notebooks offline** so you can access them when you don't have an Internet connection. This is a great feature if you are in the habit of travelling by car, train, or plane where there isn't a steady Internet connection. You can work on notebooks

offline and then synchronize them when you get a connection again.

- **Share your notebooks** and allow others to edit your notes. This is great for online collaboration, shared study, work projects, family sharing, and much more.

- **Note history.** If you accidentally delete something, or if you make a change to a document that you regret, you can go to your note history in your Evernote web account, access the note's history, and roll back to a previous version.

- You can **upload larger files** to Evernote (up to 50MB from a previous 25MB).

- **Faster image recognition.** If you have a scanned image with text or a photo with text on it, being a premium customer will get those images indexed faster by Evernote's OCR technology.

- **PIN lock.** I am a big privacy person and am also nervous that if I lose my iPad and/or iPhone on the street, the person who finds them will have complete access to everything on my phone. So the ability for premium Evernote customers to put a PIN lock on their account is invaluable.

- **PDF search.** If you are a big fan of PDF files (like me) then you will want to store them all in your Evernote account. If you're a premium customer, you will be able to make keyword searches inside those PDF files to make it easier to find a file on a specific subject.

- *Hide adverts.* Last but not least, you can hide the adverts. I personally feel that the adverts are not intrusive and you may choose to leave them alone, but as a premium customer, you have the option of switching them off.

Chapter 2 - Evernote on Your Desktop - Overview

The Notetaking Software for Your Preferred Desktop Platforms

Nowadays, people who are living in the busy stream of everyday life use various operating systems for their personal computers or laptops. From Microsoft Windows for Windows users to OS X for Mac users, Evernote brags compatibility with your chosen platform.

The latest update to the desktop application offers the following advantages:

1. User Interface (UI) that is easier to use.

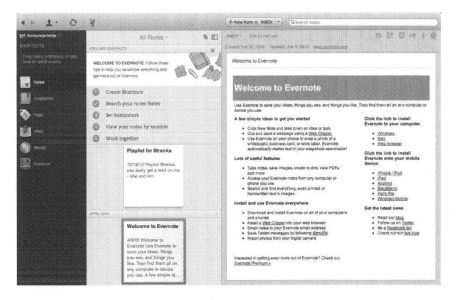

Fig. 2.1Evernote User Interface for Mac

2. The Sidebar function, for quick access to everything.

Fig 2.2 The Sidebar

3. 'Atlas' feature to search your note based on the location you created it, and group your notes around common locations.

Fig 2.3 The Atlas Feature

Getting Started with Evernote

Now that you know what Evernote can help you with, it's time to experience it yourself. In this chapter we will introduce you to the steps and concepts that will help you start remembering everything about using Evernote on your desktop.

Before starting, here are the terms that will be used over and over that help describe what Evernote consists of.

Note: A single item stored in Evernote.

Notebook: A container for notes.

Sync: The process by which your Evernote notes are kept up-to-date across all your computers, phones, devices, and the web.

Account: A username and password that allows Evernote to identify your notes and make them available to you anywhere.

Installing the Evernote Desktop Client

To be able to start using Evernote on your desktop, the first step would be to download and install the application. You can easily find the installer by searching for it on Google.

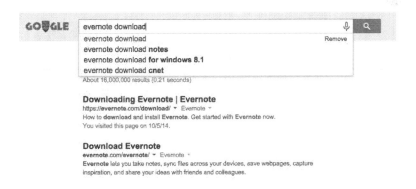

Fig 2.4 Finding Evernote installer is as easy as it can get

Getting Your Evernote User Account

If you already have an Evernote account, the new application that you install will ask you to log in to your existing account to let it sync all your notes that you already create on other platforms.

Fig 2.5 The Sign In Window

In case you are totally new to Evernote, you can click "Create an Account" and input your email address, username, and password information to get started.

Fig 2.6 Create your Evernote account to start using the application

Create Your First Note

Congratulations! Now that you are an Evernote user, you can embark on your journey for a more organized life by creating your first note. In Evernote, there are so many options of the kind of note that you can create; simple text documents, to-do lists, webpage articles to read later, recipe ideas, and many more.

To get the hang of how Evernote works, first you can create a new note by clicking the "New Note" button.

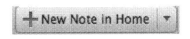

Fig. 2.7 New Note buttons

After you click it, a blank note screen will appear.

Fig 2.8 A blank note screen, ready to be modified

You can start modifying your note, starting from the title. To edit the content, you can click on the main body of the note to start adding content.

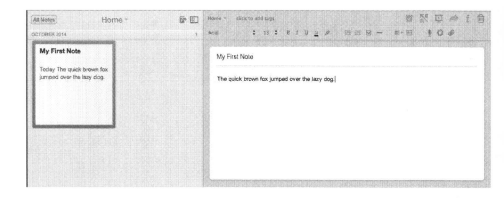

Fig. 2.9 A Sample note with modified title and content

Evernote also allows you to style the text by changing the

font, increasing or decreasing the size, changing the color, or bolding/italicizing/underlining it with the available options in the toolbar above the note body.

Personalize Your Note with Images

The fun part of Evernote is that it isn't always about storing an abundance of documents. To make your note more appealing – or just for the sake of saving the photographs of your recent gathering with old friends – you can opt to add images from your image folders.

To add a new image, simply copy the image and paste it in your new note.

Fig 2.10 Anew note with an image attached

What is Evernote Sync?

Boasting the ease of access to various gadgets you have, one of the most functional features of Evernote is its ability to synchronize all the notes that you create; it doesn't matter if you saved the sudden thought you had on your bus home from work to your phone, you can easily open and continue it later in the comfort of your home using your desktop Evernote application.

When you open the application, assuming you are always connected to the Internet for the free account users, Evernote will sync all your latest notes every once in a while. But you can always sync it manually by clicking the synchronize button at the top of the Evernote window.

Fig 2.11 The sync button is marked with the arrow cycle symbol

Saving Content While Browsing

The Internet is known as a source of vast information. With just a few keywords, you can easily find the information that you are looking for, if not more. But finding the correct information is only a part of the process. Oftentimes, you also need to save, share, and store the important article that you find, and copying and pasting the link to another platform means too much work and clutter.

Evernote simplifies this with its Web Clipper function.

Fig 2.12 The download options vary to suit your browser preference

After you search and install the Evernote Web Clipper to your web browser, every time you find the content that you want to share or read in the future, all you have to do is click the button in your browser toolbar to save it to your Evernote account.

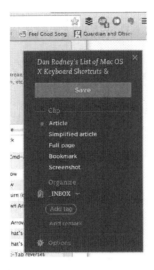

Fig 2.13 The Evernote Web Clipper window

You can choose the type of content you want to save, the folder you want to save it in, add tags for more details, and then save the content straight to your account.

Later on, you can read the content that you saved in a new note that Evernote creates for you.

Fig 2.14 A new note with the website content that you saved using Web Clipper

Need Reminders?

For more urgent and time-sensitive notes, such as your to-do list for a particular date, Evernote facilitates an in-app reminder and email notification to help you remember important tasks.

Click on the clock button at the top of your note to set a reminder.

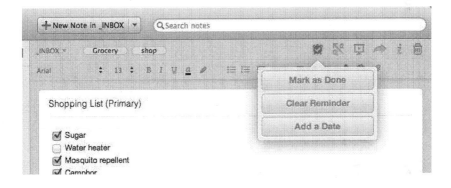

Fig 2.15 Setting a reminder is just one click away

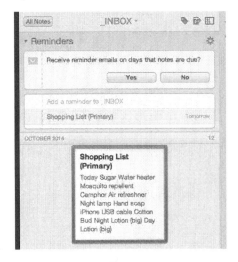

Fig 2.16 You can also opt to receive email notification for your note

The notes that you set a reminder for will appear as to-do lists at the top of your Notes list so you can monitor them easily, which means after you have finished the activities for a particular note, you can check off the reminder by clicking the checkbox.

Fig 2.16 A checked off reminder

Create Your First Webcam Note

Provided your laptop/PC has a webcam, you may encounter a new note type in your Evernote Toolbar, called WebCam note.

Fig 2.17 Evernote Window Toolbar

Clicking the WebCam note icon turns on your camera and pops open a snapshot window. You can use this feature to add images straight to your note.

Chapter 3 - Evernote on Your Handheld: An Overview

On Apple's iOS

Evernote is available across many platforms, including, of course, iOS for iPhone and iPad users. While the main application itself is updated regularly to improve its functionality and performance, using Evernote on an iOS device gives an additional advantage because there are so many companion apps that support it. These include Evernote Peek, Evernote Food, Evernote Hello, and Biscuit.

Evernote Peek

Still available for iPad only, Evernote Peek is a study tool that lets you take notes in Evernote and turn them into study material. As its unique name suggests, Evernote Peek lets you see the clue and the answer, well, by peeking through your iPad's Smart Cover or by using its virtual smart cover. A way to study that is fun and engaging at the same time, Evernote Peek also provides in-app content by professional publishers for you to learn something new and interesting.

Evernote Food

Evernote Food is Evernote itself, only specialized for storing any information about food. How trivial it may sound, you will find it useful if you ever have a hard time deciding what to eat for dinner. Evernote Food will come to the rescue as you search through the to-try list of recipes that you made using the Web Clipper.

Fig 3.1 Evernote Food Home Window

Don't fancy cooking at the moment? You can share your location and let Evernote Food discover the delicious restaurants around your neighborhood and then store pictures of your meals if you ultimately decide it's worth it.

Evernote Hello

Every day you meet new people, with their different roles and histories. In Evernote, you can treat people you meet like important information you find, in a good way. Each time you are introduced to a new person, you can scan their business card to get the essential information. Furthermore, you can also mark the calendar and location of your meeting. You no longer have to browse through unorganized stacks of business cards to contact that particular person who you met at the coffee shop near your office a few weeks ago. Evernote Hello will be your helping hand.

Fig 3.2 Choose your own way of information input

Fig 3.3 Scan the business card to get instant information

Biscuit

This incredibly useful supporting application is your best buddy for expanding your vocabulary. First, it works as storage for every new word that you find. After you save it to the Biscuit Box, you can see the definition by tapping the desired word.

Fig 3.4 No need to go back and forth to other dictionary apps

Second, the moment you save a word to Biscuit, it immediately finds the definition for you to read. The interesting part is, if you find a new word that you want to know the definition of in an online article on your mobile phone–or in your desktop browser provided you already installed Web Clipper to it–when you highlight the word and copy it, Biscuit will instantly receive the word and give you the definition through your notifications.

Biscuit's last function is its flash card feature. From the collection of new words that you input to Biscuit, the app will randomly send you selected flashcards from your Box at set times every day. The app will basically 'force' you to master a word every single day (if you want it to) until you mark it as 'Memorized.'

Creating Your First Audio Note

Too lazy to write it down and know there's no picture that can represent the thought you're having that you really need to follow up later? Then the audio note alternative in Evernote is your answer.

To make an audio note, start by first creating a new note as usual. Then to start recording, tap the microphone button.

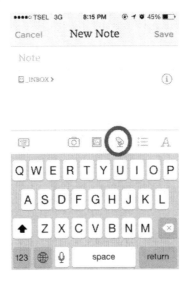

Fig 3.5 Tap the microphone button to start recording

Title your new note and tag it if necessary and your audio will be available in your Evernote account for you to access anytime.

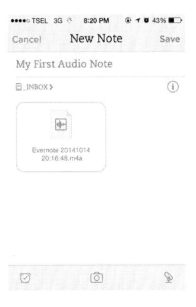

Fig 3.6 Your new audio note is created

Chapter 4 - Tips and Tricks - Making the Best of Evernote

Using the Desktop Toolbar - Important Notes at Your Fingertips

Having multiple notes in your Evernote account can be a slight disadvantage if you, for example, are currently using Evernote to develop that important essay you need to finish by next week.

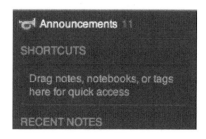

Fig 4.1 You can find Shortcuts on your Evernote desktop toolbar

To separate the important notes that you need to access easily, simply drag your chosen note to the Shortcut toolbar. Now every time you want to go into your essay, no matter where you are in the Evernote system, you can go to it directly from Shortcut.

Creating a Table of Contents in a Note

One of Evernote's features that is currently only available on Evernote Mac and Windows desktop applications is the Table of Contents. A Table of Contents in Evernote is a note with a list of links to other notes to simplify the task of searching by enabling you to just scan through the links that you made.

To create a Table of Contents, first select the multiple notes that you want to include.

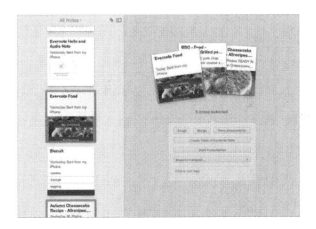

Fig 4.2Hold command(ctrl) +click to select multiple notes

As soon as you have selected multiple notes, the "Table of Contents" note menu will appear. Click it, and Evernote will make a new note consisting of the links to all the notes that you selected.

Table of Contents

1. Evernote Food
2. Autumn Cheesecake Recipe - Allrecipes.com
3. BBC - Food - Recipes : Grilled pork chop with cauliflower cheese and cabba

Fig 4.3 A new note of links is created

The next time you want to access these notes in Evernote desktop, just click on the link and the note will immediately open. You can also drag the Table of Contents to the Shortcut toolbar to further decrease the searching time for the important notes.

Adding Multiple Types of Media to a Single Note

Now that you know that Evernote can store texts, images, audio notes, and attached document files, you may start to wonder: Can Evernote store them all at once in one note? Why, yes, of course.

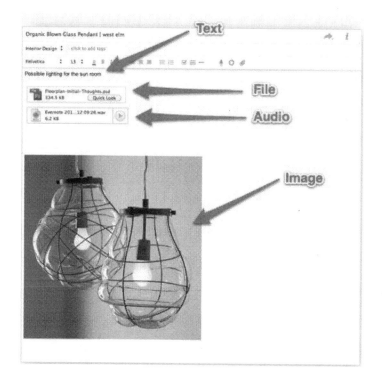

Fig 4.4 A note with texts, audio, image, and document

The steps are pretty simple, because you essentially make the standard notes that you already know how to make, just all in one single note. To input text, all you have to do is type into the note body. To add a document, drag your related document to your note. To add audio, click the record button to start recording. To add an image, simply copy and paste the desired image to the same note. And voila, now you have all the necessary information about a certain topic in the same note.

Evernote and Twitter - Saving Tweets

Being a nostalgic person like I am—and a Twitter user for years—I often read through all of my tweets to remember what I wrote in my past days. Evernote, with its great understanding of these users, has developed a way to safely store everything about your tweets (the new tweets that you post, your most recent favorite tweets, new links, and hashtags).

Previously, Evernote provided a service called @myEN that let you save tweets directly to your Evernote account. Now that that service has been shut down, you can opt to use a third-party application called IFTTT (If This Then That).

IFTTT connects two services of your choice to create an automated flow called a 'recipe'. In the case of saving your favorite tweet, create your own 'recipe' by choosing 'new favorite tweet' as 'this' and choosing 'create a note in Evernote' as 'that.'

Fig 4.5 Create a personalized flow for your chosen channel

Evernote will then create a new notebook–if not yet available–and a new note for your recent favorite tweet.

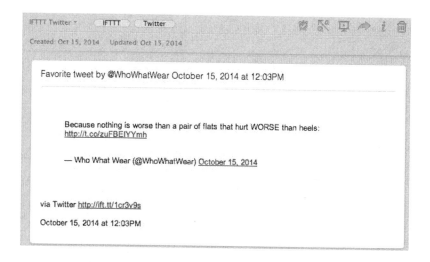

Fig 4.6 Access your tweet through Evernote

Evernote and Google+ - Saving Content

So, you are an active Google+ user and find that you posted more information there than you did on Twitter? Worry not, because IFTTT can also support your cause.

Though the process of linking your G+ account to Evernote is slightly more complicated than linking your Twitter account, you can safely store your G+ content with this simple guide:

1. Choose "Feed" as your Trigger Channel in IFTTT and choose "New feed item" as the trigger.
2. Copy your G+ profile page URL.
3. Go to http://goo.gl/5FbuL to make an automated custom URL.

Fig 4.7 Simply copy and paste your profile URL in the space provided

4. Copy the generated RSS Feed URL in Plus Channel into the URL space provided in IFTTT.

5. Finish by setting Evernote options as your Action Fields (you can change the title of the new Notebook from"RSS Feed" to "G+" if you wish).

Creating To-Do Lists

Nothing beats the satisfaction of checking off an item in a to-do list. But before checking off anything, obviously, you have to make the to-do list first. Evernote included this feature as everyone always needs to have a to-do list for something, like shopping lists, packing lists, errand lists, and many more.

To make a to-do list in Evernote, create a new note and give it a title to start with. Click the checklist icon to generate your first to-do list (an "Insert To-do" will appear if you place your pointer above the checklist icon).

Fig 4.8 Click on the icon to start making a to-do list

You can add as many checklists as needed in one note.

The Evernote Email System and Emailing into Notes

At the process of registering into your Evernote account, you were given a certain email address created from your username and some random numbers that you can save to your contact list. That was Evernote telling you that you have a dedicated email address that lets you forward emails, tweets, or any other type of content to any of your notebooks.

The gist of it is pretty simple: Whenever you need to add content to your Evernote account but don't have the access to it (example, in your office PC), you can email the content to your Evernote email address so it will be available to you later. You can even specify where you want the content to appear by typing'@'+notebook name for a specified notebook and '#'+hashtag name for a specified hashtag in your email subject line.

Forget your Evernote email address? You are able to see your custom email address in your account info for Evernote desktop users and in Settings>General >Evernote Email Address for Evernote handheld users.

Sharing your Data on Social Media (Facebook, Twitter, LinkedIn, and Email)

Now you already saved all the important notes and you want to share this certain article with your friends who might find it interesting. The arrow icon that you can find in your note toolbar is there to serve your purpose.

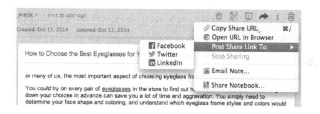

Fig 4.9 Click on the arrow icon to trigger the sharing options

You can opt to share your note to your Facebook account, Twitter account, or LinkedIn account, or just email the note to the people in your contact list if you want to be more private.

Sharing a Notebook

Sharing a whole notebook is as easy as sharing a single note. When you make a notebook containing files for your office project and need to share it with your co-workers, click the sharing icon. Simply drag your mouse to highlight your work notebook.

Fig 4.10 The sharing icon

You can decide to share the notebook with only specific people by choosing the "Share" option and invite them by their email address. Or, if you want your notebook to reach as many people as possible, use "Publish" to create a link for your notebook to be posted anywhere you want (you can also invite people using the "Publish" option).

How to Subscribe

If you grow to love Evernote and become interested in all the privileges offered to Evernote Premium users, you can start subscribing monthly/yearly by registering through your Evernote Mobile, Evernote Desktop, or Evernote Web applications. Payment methods include credit cards, PayPal, or cards from selected 7-11 stores.

Using Encryption

Privacy is sometimes critical, especially if you use Evernote to store all kinds of information that you have, including the most sensitive such as credit card info and passwords for various web accounts. Assuming that you are a free user without access to note-lock, you can use encryptions to protect your content.

Open Evernote for Mac or Evernote for Windows to use the encryption service. Then, open a note and highlight the text you wish to encrypt and right-click or control-click the highlighted text and select "Encrypt Selected Text."

Fig 4.11 Choose "Encrypt Selected Text"

Evernote will ask you to enter a passphrase into the form, so whenever you want to access or decrypt the text, you have to enter the passphrase that you registered. However, Evernote does not store your passphrase information anywhere in the application, so make sure you remember it.

Chapter 5 - More about Evernote - Add-Ons and Plugins

Searching Google and Evernote Together

If you are a Google Chrome or Mozilla Firefox user, continue reading to learn how to kill two birds with a stone; in this case, how to search a keyword in your browser address bar while also searching through the notes you made in Evernote.

In Chrome, first you have to go the Preferences (Mac) or Tools>Options (Windows) menu.Then, click on the manage button in the Default Search section (for Mac) or Basic tab (for Windows). Click to add a new search engine, and insert "Evernote.com" as the keyword "http://www.evernote.com/search?q=%s" as the URL. All that's left is when you want to search Google and Evernote at the same time, you type "evernote.com" into the search bar, press Tab, and do a search.

For Firefox users, you can click on "Organize Bookmarks"

in the Bookmark menu. Then add a new Bookmark, and insert the same link above as the location with the easy-to-remember keyword (obviously, you can just type "Evernote" as keyword). Every time you want to do a search, type the keyword you saved followed by a space and the phrase that you want to search. So easy!

Evernote Web Clipper

If you have reached this chapter, chances are you have already installed the Evernote application and gone through Chapter 3 of this guide to know how to save your Internet content using Evernote Web Clipper.

This special extension for your web browser works as a shortcut to safely keep the information that you find while you browse the Internet. Whether you want to read it again, use it as a reference for your essay, or share it with your co-workers, all you have to do is dip into Evernote where you can easily find all the information that's important to you.

Evernote Clearly

Fig 5.1EvernoteClearly download window

Evernote Clearly, as shown in Figure 6.1, is one of the browser extensions to help you get the most out of Evernote with the main function of producing a distraction-free environment to enhance your reading experience. Through Evernote Clearly, you can also highlight any section that you want and personalize your content's font, color, and size so the final product you save to Evernote is only the important information that you need.

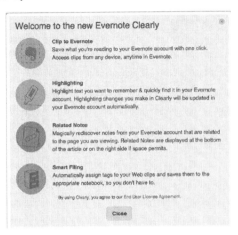

Fig 5.2 Save, modify, and organize your content with Evernote Clearly

Evernote Trunk

Starting to feel like you can do anything with Evernote yet? Hold your horses, because there is still so much to do with Evernote Trunk. Working similarly to the Appstore (for iOS) or Google Play (for Android), Evernote Trunk is an application center for anything about Evernote. If you want to expand your Evernote usage, you can browse through Evernote Trunk to search new supporting applications for your Evernote Desktop, Evernote Web, or Evernote Phone. With over 15,000 developers around the world building products and services that work with Evernote, with frequent visits to Evernote Trunk you are guaranteed to increase productivity in every aspect of your life.

Skitch

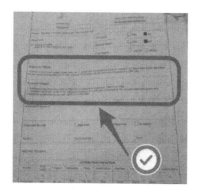

Fig 5.3 Document shared with Skitch

For some cases, images speak louder than words. Oftentimes, delivering your message through pictures and simple notes can be a hassle-free, efficient, and effective alternative when you don't have the time to arrange words just to get your intention clear.

Whether you want to share the important document with your co-worker or show your family something interesting in a landscape shot you took, all you have to do is take a picture with Skitch, add annotations/shapes/texts/sketches to get your point across with fewer words.

Using the Touch

The latest update for Windows 8, Evernote Touch, is specifically designed to run under Microsoft's new "modern" user interface (UI) on Windows 8 and RT PCs and tablets. Instead of clicking on the icons available, a Windows 8 user navigates Evernote by simply tapping them.

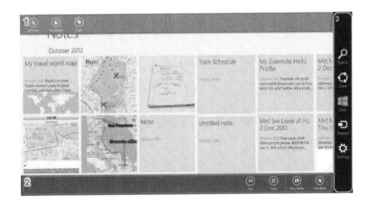

Fig 5.4Evernote Touch window

Generally providing the same service as on other platforms, Evernote Touch consists of three bars: Nav bar (1), App bar (2), Charm bar (3).

You can open existing notes, as well as create notes and

perform other account actions from the App Bar. In Evernote Touch for Windows 8 you may also use the Nav Bar to navigate to the Note List or Notebook List, and use the Charm Bar to search your Evernote account, view your account settings, and share your notes.

Evernote Ambassador Program

With the overwhelming amount of new users that are eager to know more about Evernote and make the most of it, Evernote created a global community of selected Evernote users that are experts at using Evernote in various aspects of their daily lives to show others how to follow their steps. Evernote listed all the ambassadors in the Evernote blog, each with their own specialty, along with their websites for you to learn further from their daily experiences.

Conclusion

This Evernote Beginner's Guide was written to show you how to get started exploring the basics of Evernote and to introduce you to what Evernote really is. Our goal is to give you the knowledge of what Evernote can do to help you be more organized than ever. This elementary information and instruction is essential, because we know that active people have so much information in their life, and depending on one's own memory is often not enough, while taking written notes is not always effective.

In general, Evernote is a versatile application with the main purpose of storing all kinds of information that you consider important and integrating it into many aspects of your life. You can basically do everything with Evernote; saving, presenting, sharing, reminding, and much more. You decide what you want to do to increase your potency and your ability to gain information, and let Evernote do the rest. With Evernote's vast amount of supporting applications (such as Web Clipper, Clearly, and Biscuit) and its amazing in-app features (such as Optical Character Recognition, Atlas, and the availability in multiple platforms), you are given many options and possibilities just by installing the application to one of your devices.

Nevertheless, the experience you gain is not just for yourself; Evernote makes it more meaningful by promoting the ease of sharing. Not just between the platforms that you use, but to other people through emails, social networking sites, and between Evernote users themselves, because happiness (and information!) is only real when it is shared.

Now we are at the end of the Evernote's Beginner Guide, which means you already read—and most likely practiced—all the basics of Evernote. The more you explore it, the further you can push its limitations in organizing your life. This Beginner's Guide is only the beginning of your adventure to better productivity. Are you ready to see how far you can advance your life with Evernote?

Thank you again for purchasing this book!

I hope I was able to help you to improve your productivity and master your effectiveness.

Finally, if you enjoyed this book, please take the time to share your thoughts and post a review on Amazon.

It'd be greatly appreciated.
Thank you and good luck!

BONUS: FREE Books for You

Dear reader!

If you like my books, I'd like to share more books with you **FOR FREE**.

When I set my book for free promotion, and the cost of the books is $0.00, I can send you the link for free download, and you can save up to $10 every time.

Simply follow the **link here** and let me know where to send the information about my free books.

Or simply copy this link and paste it into your browser: **http://bit.ly/1sg7oaP**

Thanks!

Allan Green

Check Out My Other Books

Below you'll find some of my other books that are popular on Amazon and Kindle as well. Simply click on the links below to check them out. Alternatively, you can visit my author page on Amazon to see more of my work.

1) Resume Writing for IT Professionals - Resume Magic or How to Find a Job with Resumes and Cover Letters

Click here to check out the book:
http://amzn.to/1JWsgZz

If the links do not work for whatever reason, you can simply search for these titles on the Amazon website to find the book.

2) Leadership Skills: Guide to Developing Leadership Skills or 7 Habits of the Leader in Me

Click here to check out the book:
http://amzn.to/1Q6hFPF

If the links do not work for whatever reason, you can simply search for these titles on the Amazon website to find the book.

3) *Your Speed Reading Guide - How to Increase Reading Speed and Read Faster, Productivity Improvement Book*

Click here to check out the book:
http://amzn.to/1c1HFgC

If the links do not work for whatever reason, you can simply search for these titles on the Amazon website to find the book.

4) *Why 90% of Startups FAIL? - Starting Small Business for Dummies, Entrepreneur Books*

Click here to check out the book:

http://amzn.to/1Je2Q9A

If the links do not work for whatever reason, you can simply search for these titles on the Amazon website to find the book.

5) *The Key To Positive Thinking - How to Be Happy and Think Positive, A Happiness Project Book*

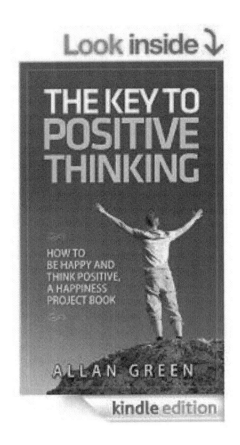

Click here to check out the book:
http://amzn.to/1EVnPQR

If the links do not work for whatever reason, you can simply search for these titles on the Amazon website to find the book.

6) Self-Confidence - How to Build Confidence and Master Conflict Management Skills

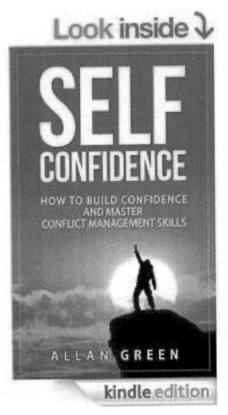

Click here to check out the book:
http://amzn.to/1AoVQBK

If the links do not work for whatever reason, you can simply search for these titles on the Amazon website to find the book.

Preview of the Book *"Power Habit - Ultimate Guide to Power of Habit, Self Control and Self Discipline"*

If you are interested in buying this book, please click here to purchase the book:

http://amzn.to/1GCwoLd

Chapter 1 Secrets to Success

Highly successful people have certain characteristics that set them apart from the rest of the crowd. You can take these traits and practice them in your life to become successful as well.

- Thinking outside the box

  They have very creative minds that help to think of innovations and new things to try. They constantly think of ways to improve or introduce new ideas. Their thinking is not confined to the limits of convention and norms.

- See challenges and difficulties as opportunities for learning and growth

  Life is not a smooth-sailing boat. Everyone will face difficulties and challenges along the way. Successful people accept these challenges and take them as an opportunity to learn what needs to change and what things need to be improved.

- Resilient- handles rejections well

  Success is not having to deal with rejections and losses. To succeed, one must learn the skill of how to be resilient and be able to work around rejections and failures.

- Driven by passion

Being passionate about one thing, about an endeavor, is a powerful driving force. Successful people are often quoted about it. Do what you love best and you will succeed.

- Finish what they started

Success is more likely with a single, finished task than hundreds of unfinished ones. Finishing one task takes you closer to your goal. Spreading yourself too thin with many unfinished tasks will get you nowhere.

- Accepts difficulties and challenges happily

Successful people happily adjust to difficulties and challenges. They accept them as avenues to test their integrity, to use skills and learn new ones, and for adventure.

- Accepts losses graciously

Success is not about never failing. In reality, successful people are those who have experienced many losses and rose above them every time. They do not become sore losers; they accept losses gladly and move on.

- Ready to take risks- fear has no hold on them

People who succeed are not those who do not

experience fear. Everyone fears something at some point in their lives. Success is achieved when you realize that these fears should not hold you back. Accept the reality of your fears and take steps to avoid these fears from becoming a reality. Fear is present in everyone, but it is only a state of mind. Learn to control fear and strive to reach your goals.

- No grudges

  Grudges use too much energy and focus that should otherwise be used to fuel success. Let go of the negative feelings. Learn to forgive and forget. When you hold grudges, you are hurting yourself instead of the other person.

- Keep positivity around them

  Successful people nurture great relationships with positive people. They have a functioning support group where they receive encouragement and constructive criticism, which helps them become better individuals.

- Don't get affected by other people's opinion of them

  You can't control what other people think about you. Their opinion is theirs and not yours. It's no use losing sleep over it.

- Not a crowd pleaser

Successful people do not live to please others.

- Get some real "me-time"

  Love yourself in order to have some love to share to others. Spend time pampering the self.

- Have routines, with exercise included in them

  Successful people develop a routine, which helps them to keep focused. Exercise is a crucial part, as with other activities. An hour, or even 15 minutes, of exercise is enough to keep the body healthy.

- Breathe deeply

  Deep breathing takes in more oxygen for the body tissues to use. More oxygen, especially to the vital organs, is necessary for mental alertness and improved mental functioning.

- Spiritual

  Health includes the spiritual side. Spend time to nurture your inner spiritual self.

- Set boundaries

  Learn to say "No" to people and stick with it. Success comes when you learn to set boundaries. People should not control how you feel and what you do.

If you are interested in buying this book, please click here to purchase the book:

http://amzn.to/1GCwoLd

Thank you!
Allan Green

23468706R00045

Made in the USA
San Bernardino, CA
18 August 2015